The Stinking Cookbook

by Jerry Dal Bozzo

(The Layman's Guide to Garlic Eating, Drinking, and Stinking)

"We Season Our Garlic With Food!"

A Celebration of Garlic and Garlic Cuisine
Made Famous by San Francisco's Most Unique Dining Experience
THE STINKING ROSE®
A Garlic Restaurant
325 Columbus Avenue, San Francisco, California

Celestial Arts
Berkeley, California

CELESTIAL ARTS
P.O. Box 7327
Berkeley, California 94707

Cover illustrations by Marlene Bauer-Holder
Text layout and illustrations by Marlene Bauer-Holder
Illustrations on page 56 and 62 by Chuck Kennedy
Photo montages on pages 60 and 74-5 by Dean Dal Bozzo

Library of Congress Cataloging-in-Publication Data
  Dal Bozzo, Jerry
    The stinking cookbook : from the Stinking Rose, a garlic restaurant / by Jerry Dal Bozzo
    p. cm.
  ISBN 0-89087-730-0
  1. Cookery (Garlic) 2. Garlic. 3. Stinking Rose (Restaurant)
I. Stinking Rose (Restaurant) II. Title.
TX819.G3D34 1994
641.6'526 — dc20   94-4157
                                                                    CIP
First Printing, 1994
        5   6
99   98   97
Manufactured in Hong Kong

THE STINKING ROSE®

A GARLIC RESTAURANT

All you have to do is follow your nose and it will lead you to one of San Francisco's most unique and entertaining dining experiences...The Stinking Rose®

Located in North Beach, San Francisco's renowned Little Italy, The Stinking Rose®: A Garlic Restaurant has become famous for celebrating the culinary euphoria of garlic and serving over 3,000 pounds of the pungent herb each month. Named after an historical term for garlic, The Stinking Rose® offers scrumptious, contemporary, California-Italian cuisine prepared and adorned with garlic and strives to accommodate every palate. There is hearty fare for the truly adventurous, mild for the novice, and *sans garlic* for those finding the herb's folklore and aroma more appealing than its taste.

And the fun goes far beyond the tantalizing choices at the table. Guests can enjoy treat after garlicky treat in any of the restaurant's whimsical dining rooms decorated with colorful garlic images, curious memorabilia and a mechanical miniature garlic factory. The world's largest garlic braid winds its way throughout the establishment, and festive murals depicting a garlic bulb's view of San Francisco's history and culture adorn the walls. The lovable bulbs, painted and brought to life by local artist Chuck Kennedy, can be found careening down The City's steep hills on skateboards, running road races and picnicking in Golden Gate Park. Garlic-shaped fish can even be seen swimming under Fisherman's Wharf. At last

count, 2,635 bulbs of garlic, two onions, and one leek festoon every conceivable nook and cranny.

The Stinking Rose® also features an extensive selection of gift and food items for take-home enjoyment. Whether you'd like to remember your visit with a colorful character t-shirt, garlic jelly, or condiments to liven up your home cooking, we have the selection for you.

Take with you a part of the restaurant that boasts the motto: "We season our garlic with food."

Have a Stinking good Time!

Why a Garlic Cookbook

Well, it's been suggested by our patrons time and time again, "Gee, you guys should really write all these great recipes down. You know, 'A Stinking Cookbook,' or something like that." We've been receiving requests like this since we first opened the restaurant, so we finally decided to get it down on paper. We accomplished what we set out to do, and the results truly stink! In the good sense, of course. We hope you'll enjoy the preparation, presentation and consumption of these recipes as much as we do — and have a good laugh at the same time.

Pay close attention to the guests you'll meet and anecdotes you'll savor along your journey through *The Stinking Cookbook*. They've been included to help make your experience educational as well as enjoyable. You'll savor these aromatic delights our way by learning to "season your garlic with food!"

Table of Contents

(Or, 36 ways to please your family and friends, but drive away your neighbors...) Here's how to find the fun, the food, and the nonsense:

How to Begin

hat's the Latin term for garlic. But don't worry! We'll stick to plain English throughout the following pages containing our wonderful garlic recipes. We don't want you to be shy, timid, or otherwise afraid about mastering the art of cooking and loving garlic. It's fun and simple, and we're here to help you along the way.

The simplest way to enjoy all of our aromatic treats is to call (415) 781-ROSE for reservations at The Stinking Rose®! But, if you insist on preparing these dishes (and serving, and cleaning up afterward) at home, this is how you should begin.

Purchasing Garlic:

Garlic's popularity spans the globe. Most of the garlic sold in the United States is grown in California, but can also be imported from Mexico and South America. At the market, you should choose bulbs that are hard and have a thin, dry, paper-like outer skin, which is usually white and tinged with pink or lavender. Avoid garlic heads that appear yellowed or are soft to the touch — these are past their prime.

Generally, the rule of thumb is the larger the clove, the more subtle the flavor. Therefore, elephant garlic, available in most markets and much larger than a regular garlic head, has many uses of its own (such as roasting), but should not be used in place of regular garlic in recipes.

Storing Garlic:

Stored in a cool, dry place, fresh garlic heads will keep for several months at a time. It's also a good idea to place them in a spot where air can circulate freely. If at all possible, don't refrigerate, as this will attract damaging moisture.

GARLIC

Preparing Garlic:

A head of garlic is actually a group of many cloves encased in a thin, papery, white skin. For preparing and cooking food, individual cloves are utilized. The number of cloves required and method of preparation will be dictated by your recipe.

To peel cloves, place each clove on a flat surface such as a cutting board. Using the flat side of a large knife, press down firmly until the papery skin breaks away from the fleshy meat of the clove. Perform this task gently if your cloves are to be sliced.

Next, you'll need to press, mince, chop, or slice your peeled cloves, and this method will again be dictated by the type of dish you're preparing. The degree of desired garlic flavor depends upon the size of the cut — the smaller the cut, the stronger and more pronounced the flavor. Smaller cuts (pressed or minced) also blend with other ingredients more quickly than large ones, especially when heated. Therefore, smaller cuts should be used in preparing recipes that require a short cooking time, or none at all. Larger cuts (coarsely chopped or sliced) should be used in dishes cooked with moderate heat over a longer period of time, which allows the flavor to mellow slowly.

A simple sauté (or, how to practice until perfect):

Most vegetables can be turned into a zesty side dish with a little olive oil and garlic — bellissimo! Preparation is also a great way to begin practicing the art and folly of garlic cookery and gauging the preferred amount and intensity of the herb. For the purposes of this little cooking tutorial, we've chosen to sauté a large bunch of fresh spinach (one of the vegetables that tastes best when prepared this way).

Lightly steam or parboil a large bunch of fresh spinach that's been soaked briefly and washed thoroughly. (Fresh spinach can harbor a lot of dirt.) While the spinach is still a vibrant, deep green color, remove from water or steam, drain well, and then transfer to a large skillet to which approximately 2 tablespoons of extra virgin olive oil have been added. Sauté the spinach at medium to high heat for about 30 seconds, stirring constantly, until all the leaves have been thoroughly heated and coated with the olive oil. Next, push the spinach to one side of the skillet, while holding it at an angle, allowing the oil to collect down at the bottom of the opposite end of the pan. To this hot oil, add two cloves of fresh, minced garlic, salt, and pepper to taste. Allow the garlic to simmer for about 10 seconds in the pool of oil, and then return the skillet to the burner, blend the mixture, and continue to sauté the vegetable, oil and garlic. Sauté the mixture until the garlic becomes translucent and golden, but not brown. (Browning will cause the garlic to become bitter, and likely spoil your recipe.) Remove spinach from the skillet and serve hot.

Easy, wasn't it...
Are you ready for more?

Garlicspeak of the World

*N*o matter how you say it (or try to say it), and no matter how it sounds, it always smells the same. For the purposes of the recipes featured on the following pages and to keep things easier for all of us, we'll always refer to garlic in Inglese (that means in English). But, in case you were wondering, here is how people around the world have named that wonderful, pungent, and most widely used herb.

Afrikaans	knoflok (knoffel)
Albanian	hudher
Arabic	tum (varies with location)
Basque	baratxuri
Danish	hvidlog
Esperanto	ajlo
Estonian	kuusauk
Finnish	laukka (or sipulitava)
French	ail
German	knoblauch
Italian	aglio
Hawaiian	aka`akai-pilau
Icelandic	knapplaukar
Irish	galrleog
Japanese	niniku
Latvian	kiploki
Lithuanian	chesnakas
Magyar	fokhagyma
Malay	bawang poetih
Maltese	tewm
Norwegian	lok
Polish	czosnok
Portuguese	alho
Rumanian	usturoiu
Russian	chesnok
Spanish	ajo
Swedish	vitlok
Ukrainian	chasnik
Welsh	garlleg
Yiddish	der knobl

Roasted Garlic

Great beginnings — a subtle way to make an immediate impact!
"And scorne not garlicke like to some that thinke. It only makes men winke, and drinke, and stinke."
Sir John Harrington
"The Englishman's Doctor" 1607

It's a hearty starter, and more tame than you might think! Perfect for the "adventuresome novice" and especially wonderful when served with crusty bread.

Serves 6
Ingredients:
6 large   heads of garlic
2 tbsp.   extra virgin olive oil
to taste   salt and pepper

Preparation:
1. Remove outer skin of garlic heads and cut tops ¼ inch so that the cloves are exposed.
2. Place cut side up in a small ovenproof casserole, drizzle with oil, season with salt and pepper, and cover with aluminum foil.
3. Bake at 325° for 1½ hours, then remove.
4. Cloves should be soft and spreadable. Serve with toasted crusty bread and brie cheese or use as an ingredient in other recipes.

Garlic Bread

An all-time favorite in our home. Garlic bread is not only a great beginning, but also great from the middle to the end — a flavorful and hearty complement to any of our "stinking" entrees, soups, or stews.

Serves 4 – 6
Ingredients:
2 tbsp.   freshly chopped garlic
4 oz.   butter
1 loaf   french bread
½ oz.   grated parmesan cheese

Preparation:
1. Place garlic and butter in food processor, and process until combined.
2. Cut french bread into two halves, lengthwise.
3. Spread each half with the garlic butter mixture.
4. Sprinkle with cheese.
5. Bake in 350° oven until lightly browned.

Garlic Pizza

*T*he origin of pizza has been debated so often we're not going to bother with it here. We know it's Italian, and what do the Greeks know, anyway? This appetizer version was so popular at The Stinking Rose® we just had to include it in our Great Beginnings. If you really want to learn how to make our other varieties of *pizzette*, you're going to have to watch our chef prepare them at our restaurant (if he'll let you), or figure it out for yourself!

Makes 4 4" Pizzas

Pizza Dough

Ingredients:

1 package	active dry yeast
1 1/4 cups	warm water
1/2 cup	olive oil
3-3 1/2 cups	all-purpose flour
1 tsp.	salt

Preparation:

1. Soften the yeast in water.
2. Stir in the oil then the flour and salt.
3. Knead until the dough is smooth and elastic — 15–20 minutes.
4. Place dough in an oiled bowl and cover with plastic wrap.
5. Refrigerate for 1 hour.

Garlic Pizza

Ingredients:

1	recipe for pizza dough
4 tbsp.	olive oil
4 tbsp.	chopped fresh garlic
8 oz.	grated smoked mozzarella
1/2 cup	chopped fresh basil

Preparation:

1. Preheat oven to 500°. Put a sheet pan or pizza stone in the oven.
2. Divide the dough into 4 pieces.
3. Roll each piece into a 6-inch circle.
4. Stretch each circle another 2 inches by hand.
5. Brush each circle with olive oil and spread with chopped garlic.
6. Top with cheese.
7. Place pizzas in oven and bake for 5–7 minutes.
8. Remove pizzas and sprinkle with fresh basil.

Gilroy:
The Garlic Capital of the World

©1979 G.G.F.A. Inc.

The very "root" of our inspiration, where it all began, and one heck of a "stinky" town: Gilroy, The Garlic Capital of the World.

Gilroy, California, the undisputed Garlic Capital of the World, grows, processes, and ships millions of pounds of garlic and garlic products each year.

Located at the intersection of Highways 101 and 152, eighty miles south of San Francisco, Gilroy takes its name from a Scottish sailor, John Gilroy. In 1814, Gilroy was put ashore in nearby Monterey after falling ill with scurvy. He settled a short distance to the east from that site, and is remembered as California's first non-Spanish settler.

Every summer, to celebrate Gilroy's "King of Flavors" and "The Stinking Rose," Gilroyans host the Gilroy Garlic Festival. A myriad of activities and "garlicky" exhibits are featured, including gourmet cooks demonstrating the preparation of delightful recipes enhanced with garlic.

This event is a must for all garlic worshippers!

Photos by Bill Strange

Baked Brie

If you really want to do it up right, (the cheese, that is), try this honey of a recipe that's the perfect accompaniment to our roasted garlic. Add some fruit, such as crisp red apple slices or grapes. An "appetizing" combination!

Serves 4
Ingredients:

1 recipe	Pizza Dough (see recipe p. 11)
1	wedge or small wheel of brie cheese
2 tbsp.	honey
1 head	Roasted Garlic (see recipe p. 9)
1 loaf	crusty french bread

Preparation:

1. Place the brie on pizza dough portions and spread honey evenly over all. Fold dough in half, over cheese; pinch edges closed.

2. Place in a 450° oven for 10 minutes or until brie is soft.

3. Serve with roasted garlic and french bread.

Bagna Calda

*T*his is our version of Italian fondue — great for parties, or a sizzling treat for two. In the Old Country, Bagna Calda (or Bagna Cauda, to some) is a popular holiday dish, served as an appetizer with a variety of simple foods for easy dipping and munching. The simmering olive oil used in our recipe creates a natural poaching process, rendering the garlic cloves soft and spreadable on fresh sourdough bread (obviously, the San Francisco favorite) or crackers. Also, it's easy to boast to your friends at the table, "watch while I swallow whole cloves in one bite." Guaranteed to impress every time . . .

Sourdough bread, crackers, or bread sticks, and a variety of cooked, sliced vegetables are perfect accompaniments to the sizzling, fragrant oil mixture. For dipping vegetables, we suggest bell peppers, carrot sticks, zucchini, broccoli, cauliflower and whole mushrooms. (But, feel free to use your imagination!)

Serves 6
Ingredients:

1 ½ cups	peeled garlic cloves
1 ½ cups	extra virgin olive oil
2 oz.	butter
1	can (2 oz.) anchovies

Preparation:

1. Place all ingredients in oven casserole, cover and place in 275° oven for 1 ½ hours.
2. Serve with bread and cut up vegetables.

*M*any varieties of clams and other types of fish and shellfish have been staples in Italian cooking since the times of the early Roman feasts. It's no wonder, since the country is nearly surrounded by bodies of water. Since that first day when someone exclaimed, "Hey, let's go fishing!", we've been blessed with the bounty known to Italians, here and abroad, as *frutti di mare*. It's shellfish to the landlubbers, and the basis for many a succulent dish in this book and in our restaurant. *Buon Gusto*!

Great Beginnings
Steamed Clams

Serves 4

Ingredients:

3–4 lbs.	Manila or small cherrystone clams
2 tbsp.	freshly chopped garlic
2 cups	fish stock or clam juice
1/2 cup	dry white wine
3 oz.	butter
1/2 cup	chopped fennel
1 pinch	saffron

Preparation:

1. Soak clams in water to remove any sand.
2. Place all ingredients in a large stock pot.
3. Cook over high heat until clams open.
4. Spoon into bowls with the broth. Serve with crusty bread.

*A*nd now, a brief visit with one of San Francisco's most notable, historic landmarks. (Certainly one not found on any tourist map of our famed city...)

LAW OFFICES OF

BELLI

The Belli Building
722 Montgomery Street
San Francisco, California 94111

(Temporary Earthquake Address: 574 Pacific, San Francisco, CA 94133)

August 13, 1991

The Stinking Rose
325 Columbus Avenue
San Francisco, CA 94133

Dear Friends and Gourmet Glutton Dinners:

Thank God now we've got a restaurant in San Francisco that will satiate our gluttony appetites and guarantee us good health -- the salubrious ministrations of garlic!

If garlic were just invented some of these extravagant advertisers would be "the first to make the extravagant claims we now know are true ... that next to sex, garlic does the most for longevity -- except a good lawyer!"

Long may your restaurant survive and the aromatic goodness of garlic pervade the salubrious foggy air of San Francisco.

I now know where and when to come if depression should ever strike and I have lost all my Prozac.

We'll be seeing (not suing) you soonest and frequently.

God bless, good luck, and good health.

Very truly yours,

MELVIN M. BELLI, SR.
The King of Torts

MMB/lw

P.S. I am issuing an edict to all of my subjects in my kingdom to visit you soon and often and to order all of your magnificent dishes, "double strength".

Garlic Caesar Salad

It's the "King of Salads" (Quite possibly the favorite dish of The City's senior "King of Torts," Mr. Belli.)

It was originally grown and cultivated in central Asia, but garlic's popularity (and odor, we assume) soon spread throughout the Middle East, and became a popular food and medicinal healer among the Hebrew, Egyptian, and other neighboring cultures. And, true to what we've learned about the character of these ancient civilizations, once the Hebrews and Egyptians had it, the Greek and Roman empires had to get in on it, too. In Greece, the Olympic athletes were fed heads of raw garlic to increase their strength. In Rome, well . . . the Romans decided to use it to make a salad, and they named it after one of their legendary leaders.

(Well, maybe not, but it still makes for a great story!)

Serves 4–6
Ingredients:

2 heads	romaine lettuce
1 tsp.	minced fresh garlic
6	canned anchovy fillets, mashed or pureed
2	egg yolks, beaten
1 tsp.	Dijon mustard
¼ cup	fresh lemon juice
½ cup	freshly grated parmesan cheese
⅓ cup	olive oil
20	freshly baked croutons
1 tsp.	freshly ground white pepper

Preparation:

1. Wash the lettuce and remove all outer leaves.
2. Keep the leaves long, or cut into large squares, whichever you prefer.
3. Spin or wipe leaves dry.
4. In a large salad bowl mix the garlic, anchovy, eggs, mustard, lemon juice and parmesan.
5. Add the lettuce, olive oil and croutons and mix well.
6. Add white pepper and continue to mix.
7. Serve and top with shaved parmesan.

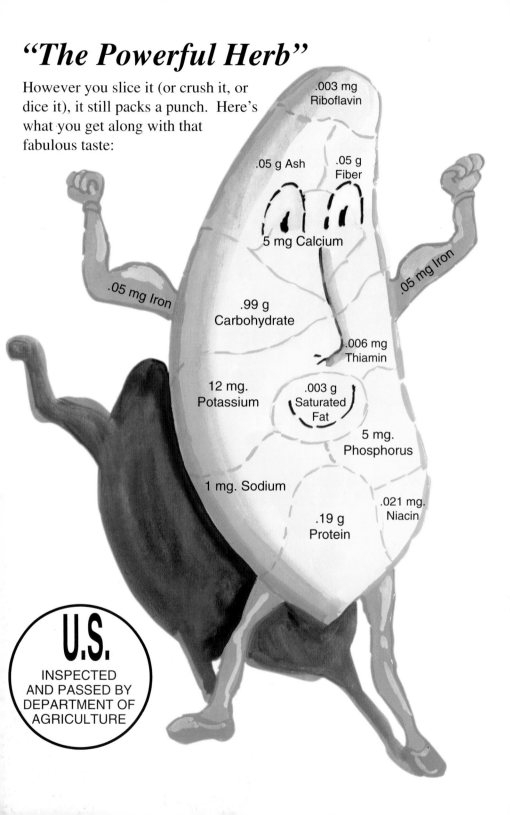

"The Powerful Herb"

However you slice it (or crush it, or dice it), it still packs a punch. Here's what you get along with that fabulous taste:

.003 mg Riboflavin

.05 g Ash

.05 g Fiber

5 mg Calcium

.05 mg Iron

.05 mg Iron

.99 g Carbohydrate

.006 mg Thiamin

12 mg. Potassium

.003 g Saturated Fat

5 mg. Phosphorus

1 mg. Sodium

.021 mg. Niacin

.19 g Protein

U.S. INSPECTED AND PASSED BY DEPARTMENT OF AGRICULTURE

Great Beginnings
Artichoke Soup

"Let good fortune (and soup) poureth over."

Old Italian proverb

*F*orget the coins, but make a wish that soup this good will never be out of reach! Soup, another Italian fundamental, made its way to many traditional North Beach dining tables to welcome the weary men home from a day's work, or to tantalize taste buds as a first course at ceremonial Sunday dinners. We've "spiced" up our modern version, and made the preparation easier (we'll bet Mamma wished she'd had a food processor!). But, it would still warm her heart, as it does ours!

Artichokes are also a plentiful, locally grown favorite in San Francisco, and baby artichokes are extremely tender and delicious.

Serves 6
Ingredients:

3 cans	water-packed artichoke hearts
2 med.	chopped onions
3 sprigs	fresh thyme
2	whole bay leaves
4 cups	chicken stock
to taste	salt
1/2 cup	roasted garlic puree
1 cup	heavy cream
4 oz.	grated monterey jack cheese

Preparation:
1. Cut artichokes in half, place in pot with onions, thyme, bay leaves, and chicken stock. Add salt, and bring to a boil. Cook until artichokes are very soft.
2. Puree the soup, using either a hand held blender or a food processor.
3. Strain, or pass through food mill.
4. Return soup to pot, bring to a simmer, then add the roasted garlic, cream and the cheese. Whip until smooth and cheese is incorporated.
5. Adjust seasoning with salt and pepper, and serve.

Great Beginnings
Green Garlic Soup

Springtime signals the coming of green garlic, which resembles green onion and is generally available for a short time during this season. This "baby garlic" is plucked before it has a chance to mature but still boasts an "adult" garlic taste! The chopped, tender shoots used in our Green Garlic Soup make a hearty and tangy broth for garlic connoisseurs of all ages.

Serves 6
Ingredients:

2 oz.	butter
4 bunches	green garlic, cleaned and roughly chopped
3	potatoes, peeled and quartered
6 cups	chicken stock or canned chicken broth
to taste	salt and white pepper
1 cup	heavy cream

Preparation:

1. In a large pot, melt the butter and sauté the green garlic.
2. Add the potatoes and the chicken stock. Cover and bring to a simmer.
3. Cook for 30 minutes.
4. Puree the soup in a blender or food processor and pass through a fine strainer.
5. Season with salt and pepper; add cream.
6. Serve with Garlic Croutons (see recipe p. 63).

Garlic Chowder

Serves 6 – 8
Ingredients:

2 oz.	olive oil
4 oz.	bacon, diced (optional)
2 med.	onions, diced
1/2 head	celery, diced
1 bunch	fresh leeks, cleaned and chopped
5 heads	Roasted Garlic (see recipe p. 9)
2 tbsp.	fresh thyme
3 med.	potatoes, peeled and diced
6 cups	chicken stock
to taste	salt and white pepper
1 cup	heavy cream (optional)
1/2 cup	chopped fresh parsley

Preparation:

1. In a large pot, heat the olive oil.
2. Sauté the bacon and add the onions, celery and leeks.
3. Remove the roasted garlic cloves from the head by squeezing the roasted head. Add cloves to the pot.
4. Add thyme, potatoes and chicken stock.
5. Bring to a simmer and cook until potatoes are tender (about 30 minutes).
6. Season with salt and pepper.
7. Add cream and parsley. Remove from heat and serve.

We've made this dish a true "family affair" — the *Allium* family, that is. Along with the savory onions, leeks, and, of course, garlic, the *Allium* family also includes about 600 bulb-like relatives and in-laws. (Wow, that must be one heck of a family portrait!)
Well, these three major family members, who get along most famously, have joined hands and tastes here to help us create a creamy, fragrant chowder that will be well received at *your* next family get together.

OFF TO A GREAT START

ppetizers traditionally are savored slooooowly, to whet and entice diners' appetites before the meal's entree is served, and what could be more easy to enjoy slooooowly than escargot! (That's the French way, and elegant way, to pronounce "snails.") And OUR way (The Stinking Rose® way) is the best way to serve them! We've delicately seasoned them with red wine and shallots, wrapped them snugly in our fabulous Pizza Dough, and then blanketed them with a savory, garlicky butter sauce. Very cozy! (And delicious!)

Escargot Calzone

Serves 4
Ingredients:

1 tbsp.	shallots, chopped
2 cups	red wine
24 large	french snails
1	recipe Pizza Dough (see recipe p. 11)
1 cup	Escargot Butter (see below)
1	egg white
¼ tsp.	salt

Preparation:
1. Place shallots and red wine in a saucepan and reduce to a syrup. Toss the drained snails in the red wine glaze.
2. Follow recipe for Pizza Dough on p. 11.
3. Place 6 snails and ¼ cup of the Escargot Butter in the center of each round.
4. Brush the edge of each round with egg white.
5. Fold like a turnover or half moon and seal the edge with a fork.
6. Brush top with egg white and sprinkle with salt.
7. Place on baking sheet and bake at 500° for 10 minutes.

Escargot Butter
Ingredients:

8 oz.	butter
2 tbsp.	freshly chopped garlic
1 tbsp.	chopped shallot
2 tbsp.	fresh tarragon
4 tbsp.	chopped parsley
1 tbsp.	champagne vinegar
to taste	salt and pepper

Preparation:
1. Combine all ingredients in the food processor and blend until smooth.

Being the "great thinkers" that we are, we think (actually, we're sure) that our "Main Event" dishes will become the focal point of any great, garlicky meal you prepare at home. We've included the most popular selections from our restaurant, plus some family favorites for good measure...

A lean cut of beef, fresh herbs and spices, and a "kick" of cognac make this dish one heck of a hearty steak! Be sure to couple this main course with our crispy Garlic French Fries or Creamy Garlic Mashed Potatoes and, of course, a full-bodied Italian red wine. And, if dining by candlelight, don't let the fire get too close to this dish — it's already a hot one! Our first recipe...

Garlic Filet Mignon

Serves 4
Ingredients:

4	8 oz. filet mignons
to taste	salt and freshly ground black pepper
2 tbsp.	extra virgin olive oil
4 tbsp.	butter
2 tbsp.	chopped fresh garlic
1 tbsp.	chopped shallots
2 tbsp.	chopped fresh parsley
1 tbsp.	fresh thyme
1 tbsp.	fresh tarragon
2 oz.	cognac

Preparation:

1. With the palm of your hand or the bottom of a skillet, flatten the filets to ¾ inch high.
2. Season both sides well with salt and pepper.
3. Heat a thick skillet over high heat.
4. Add the olive oil and 1 tbsp. butter.
5. When butter is brown, add the filet. Cook about 2 minutes on each side.
6. Remove the filets and place on plate.
7. Discard excess grease from the skillet.
8. Add garlic, shallots and herbs to skillet and sauté.
9. Remove from heat and add cognac after 30 seconds. Return to low heat and add remaining butter.
10. Stir mixture to form sauce and pour over filets.

29

Garlic Rose

Penne Putanesca

s history (or legend, to be safe) has it, this dish became popular among the Italian "Ladies of the Night," who gathered at late night trattorias to enjoy this hearty meal after a long night's "work." We hope we're not being TOO presumptuous by inviting you to prepare and savor this notorious feast in the comforts of your own home.

It may have you dancing in the streets!

Serves 4
Ingredients:

4 oz.	extra virgin olive oil
2 tbsp.	freshly chopped garlic
1 tbsp.	freshly chopped shallots
to taste	salt and pepper
3 cups	ripe tomatoes, peeled, seeded and chopped
6	canned anchovy filets, chopped or mashed
3 tbsp.	capers
½ cup	chopped green olives
1 tsp.	crushed red chili pepper
¼ cup	chopped fresh basil
12 oz.	penne pasta
to taste	freshly grated parmesan cheese

Preparation:
1. In a large skillet, heat the olive oil.
2. Add the garlic and shallots, and sauté. Add salt and pepper to taste.
3. Add the tomatoes and sauté for 1 minute.
4. Add anchovies, capers, olives, chili and basil. Reduce heat. Cook for 15 minutes.
5. Cook the penne in salted boiling water until *al dente*. Drain well.
6. Add pasta to the sauce and toss.
7. Serve in bowls. Top with parmesan.

Garlic — m...
favorite
aphrodisi...
Senator
Quentin L. ...

We rest our case!

Garlic has been known to make the heart go pitter-patter — but is it *amore*? Only you will know for sure . . . if it brings a song to your heart, raise your glass, belt out a tune and enjoy! "Drink to me only with "swine" eyes . . ."

If our Italian ancestors were not fisherman, they were probably the farmers who helped carry on a long tradition of raising livestock which ended up in Italian kitchens as a wide variety of cuts of meat. If pork was not swiftly transformed into luscious spicy or sweet sausage, it became a succulent roast or skillet of chops.

Although many Italian pork dishes favor lemon as the perfect fruit accompaniment, we've "Americanized" our dish to feature the ever-present apples-with-pork. Of course, we've also "garlicked" it to the nines!

Garlic Roasted Pork Chop

Garlic Roasted Pork Chop
Serves 4
Ingredients:

4	center-cut loin pork chops
1	Garlic Marinade (see recipe p. 63)
to taste	salt and white pepper
4 oz.	butter

Preparation:
1. Marinate pork chops in garlic marinade overnight.

2. Drain off chops and discard liquid. Season with salt and pepper.
3. Heat a heavy skillet, melt butter until brown.
4. Brown pork chops; put in 400° oven until done.
5. When cooked, serve on a bed of Caramelized Apples (see below) and top with Garlic Rose Relish (see recipe p. 67).

Caramelized Apples
Ingredients:

3 oz.	butter
6 oz.	sugar
4	Granny Smith apples, peeled, cored and thinly sliced

Preparation:
1. In a heavy skillet, melt butter and sugar over high heat.
2. Add the apples and let cook until sugar starts to brown.
3. Turn the apples with a spoon and continue to cook until all apples are browned.

*Y*ou're really "on the road" to preparing "a real hit" (O.K., no more bad jokes!) for your family or dinner guests with this very special Stinking Rose creation.

(We'll let the pictures speak for themselves — but please don't misinterpret their presence as a serving suggestion!)

Braised Rabbit

Serves 4

Ingredients:

1/2 cup	extra virgin olive oil
2	fresh rabbits, cleaned and cut into pieces
1/2 cup	flour
to taste	salt and pepper
2	chopped onions
3/4 cup	fresh mushrooms, quartered
3/4 cup	chopped pancetta or thick bacon
1/2 cup	chopped green olives
2 cups	chopped tomatoes, canned or freshly peeled
1 cup	whole garlic cloves, peeled
1/4 cup	red wine vinegar
2 cups	dry red wine
2 cups	chicken stock
3 sprigs	fresh thyme

Preparation:

1. Heat a large skillet with olive oil.
2. Dredge the rabbit with flour and season with salt and pepper.
3. Brown the rabbit in the skillet.
4. Add all other ingredients.
5. Bring to a simmer and place in a 350° oven for 1 1/2 hours uncovered in the skillet.

Cioppino

*A*s history tells us, Cioppino was a hearty fish stew that sustained San Francisco's Sicilian fishermen during their long days and nights scouring the sea and the bay for the best catch. It kept them warm at night, and supposedly chased away colds and other illnesses.

Our version ain't your Mamma's "chicken soup," but it will probably cure what ails ya—even if you've just got a yearning for seafood. And if it is, this dish is certainly the right prescription. Fresh fish, shrimp, clams, mussels, crabs, and scallops—our Cioppino has cornered the fish market on fish. What more could you ask for! (Go ahead and throw in that lobster tail, if you must — but we don't recommend it!)

"Try this, some crusty bread and a bottle of Chianti—but don't call us in the morning!"

Serves 6–8
Ingredients

2 lbs.	firm fresh filet (snapper, bass, swordfish)
10–12	large shrimp (preferably fresh, with head on)
18–20	Manila clams
18–20	mussels
1	Dungeness crab, cooked, cleaned and cracked
10–12	medium to large sea scallops
1 tbsp.	minced garlic
1 tbsp.	minced shallots
4 oz.	butter
¼ tbsp.	orange zest
¼ tbsp.	saffron
¼ bunch	chopped fresh basil
1 qt.	marinara sauce
3 cups	fish stock or clam juice
1 cup	white wine

Preparation:

1. Cut the fish filet into cubes. Remove all bones.
2. Wash all shellfish. Remove shells from shrimp if you prefer them shelled.
3. Place all fish in a large pot or casserole.
4. Add all other ingredients.
5. Cook over high heat until mussels and clams open, approximately 10–15 minutes, covered.
6. Serve over warm Polenta (see recipe p. 55).

"Loved It"..."Hated It"... our famous friends can't decide whether or not the distinctively wonderful taste of garlic is a winner. But your own verdict will certainly be in after savoring the taste and heady aroma of this dish that's baked, garnished and presented with garlicky concoctions. Help defend our case! We'll let you be the

Braised Garlic Lamb Shanks

Serves 4
Ingredients:

¹/₂ cup	olive oil
4	lamb shanks
to taste	salt and freshly ground black pepper
1 cup	finely chopped carrots
1 cup	finely chopped fennel or celery
1 cup	finely chopped onions
2 cups	peeled garlic cloves
4 sprigs	fresh thyme or 2 tsp. dried thyme
2	bay leaves
2 cups	dry red wine
4 cups	veal or beef stock

Preparation:

1. Heat olive oil in a skillet.
2. Season the shanks with salt and pepper and brown on all sides.
3. Place browned shanks in ovenproof casserole.
4. Cover with carrots, fennel, onions, garlic, and herbs.
5. Add wine and stock and bring to a boil on stove.
6. Cover and place in a 350° oven.
7. Check shanks after 3 hours. If tender, remove from oven.
8. Serve shanks with Garlic Mashed Potatoes (see p. 45). Cover with sauce and vegetables from the pan after skimming fat, and top with Gremolata (see below).

Gremolata
Ingredients:

¹/₂ cup	chopped parsley
2 tbsp.	chopped fresh lemon peel
1 tbsp.	chopped fresh garlic

Preparation:

1. Mix all ingredients.
2. Serve over lamb shanks.

People sure do love our crab!

Garlic Roasted Whole Dungeness Crab

h, Fisherman's Wharf. A romanticist's version of heaven, and the Italian fisherman's bounty in the New World. Throughout the late 1800s and into the early 1900s, all breeds of Italian seafarers became known as "the men of Italy Harbor." Much was written about these tough pescatori, with their sea-weathered faces and full black mustaches, who set sail for their day's or week's work from the numerous piers which dotted the colorful, bustling waterfront.

By either account, fact or fantasy, these hearty men braved the treacherous waters just outside the Golden Gate to bring in the largest of the succulent Dungeness crabs, and spawned a tradition of San Franciscans craving the tender meat of this crustacean that's as popular today as it was at the turn of the century. You can still stroll along the Wharf and purchase a fresh, cracked crab or walk-away cocktail, but gone are the days of the five-cent glass of beer and all the crab legs you could eat for free!

Times have changed, and so have the many ways of preparing this delectable, local favorite (both for the better, we hope). Well, here's a salute to those days of yore, with a new, modern twist. Relish this garlicky, crabby creation, and tip your hat to those pescatori who started it all.

Serves 1

Ingredients:

1	cooked Dungeness crab	1 tbsp.	crushed red chili pepper
4 cups	extra virgin olive oil	2 tbsp.	fresh thyme
1/2 cup	chopped fresh garlic	2 tbsp.	fresh tarragon
3 tbsp.	salt	2 tbsp.	chopped parsley
1 tbsp.	freshly ground white pepper	1 cup	fresh lemon juice

Preparation:

1. Remove top shell of crab and clean the shell.
2. Prepare marinade by combining all other ingredients.
3. Leave crab in marinade for 4 hours.
4. Heat oven to 450°.
5. Place crab in large skillet with 1/2 cup of the marinade.
6. Roast in oven 15–20 minutes.
7. Serve with pan drippings.

THE GARLIC RAP SONG

(RECIPE)

The Stin-king Rose   is in ev-erything from sauces to mixes

It's bite'-ll make you sing The Stin-king Rose is in every

cul ture all peoples know it helps your composure Gar-lic

The Stin-king Rose   Gar-lic   your nose

knows

The Ro-mans knew the po-wer of the bulb they ate it in the raw

be-fore they would show   up in battle be-fore the

en-e-my it gave them the edge to fight with in-ten-si-ty

Gar-lic   The Stin-king Rose   Gar-lic

your-nose knows now that you know a-bout The Stin-king Rose

recipes   is what you want   we   su-ppose.

40 Clove Garlic Chicken

Are you still singing? Or at least "whistling while you work?" Our song may not have made the "Top 40" pop charts this week, but it's great entertainment while preparing and enjoying our "40 Clove Garlic Chicken." You heard it right. 40 cloves! But don't let that number scare you, because they add just the right amount of zest and aroma to make this one of The Stinking Rose's® most popular dishes!

Serves 4–6
Ingredients:

1 tbsp.	butter
2 tbsp.	extra virgin olive oil
2–3 lbs.	roasting chicken, washed and cut into pieces
to taste	salt and freshly ground white pepper
4 tbsp.	fresh rosemary
1 cup	flour
40	large peeled garlic cloves
1 cup	dry white wine
4 cups	chicken stock
½ cup	heavy cream

Preparation:

1. Heat the butter and olive oil in a deep, heavy skillet.
2. Season the chicken with salt, pepper, and rosemary. Toss in flour.
3. When the pan is hot, but not smoking, add the chicken, skin side down.
4. Sauté chicken until golden brown on both sides. Remove from pan.
5. Add garlic cloves and sauté until light brown.
6. Add white wine and chicken stock. Return chicken to pan.
7. Cover and simmer for 30 minutes.
8. Remove chicken and keep warm. Turn heat to high and reduce liquid by 66%. Remove to blender, add cream and puree sauce. Adjust seasoning and serve over chicken.

What's wrong with garlic?

1. Uh....

Garlic Mashed Potatoes

r, what helps make The Main Event such a big deal — these stinkingly good side dishes play superb supporting roles and are award contenders in our great garlic side dish category! Serve these up and have your guests cast their ballots …

Serves 4–6
Ingredients:

4	russet potatoes, peeled and diced
2	turnips, peeled and diced
1 cup	peeled garlic cloves
1/3 cup	heavy cream
2 oz.	butter
to taste	salt and freshly ground white pepper

Preparation:

1. Place potatoes, turnips and garlic in a large saucepan and cover with water.
2. Salt the water and bring to a boil, cooking until soft.
3. Heat the cream and the butter in a small saucepan.
4. Empty the potatoes, turnips and garlic into a colander, and let stand until well drained.
5. Place in a mixer (or use a hand mixer) and beat the potatoes with a wire whisk attachment. Add cream and butter and mix until smooth. Season with salt and pepper.

Garlic French Fries

esides our creamy Garlic Mashed Potatoes, this is our other "favorite" garlicky potato side-dish creation that's the perfect partner for many of our "Main Event" recipes (or, just a lip-smacking, finger-licking, stinkingly good snack by itself). You may want to skip the catsup. The flavor stands alone!

Serves 4
Ingredients:

4	russet potatoes, peeled and cut into 2 x 1/2-inch lengths
1 qt.	vegetable oil for frying
2	cloves chopped garlic
to taste	garlic salt

Preparation:

1. Heat oil to 325°.
2. Cook potatoes in oil and remove before they start to brown.
3. Spread on paper towel and refrigerate until cold.
4. When needed, refry with chopped garlic.
5. Add garlic salt. Toss and serve.

*H*ey, paisano—I don't got to show you no Stinking Roses, but I can show you a stinkingly good bowl of chili that's the best in the West, and I'm not blowing smoke! Whether you're north or south of the border, you're sure to enjoy this hot and hearty version of an all-time favorite. We make ours special by adding savory chunks of lamb, freshly chopped garlic and whole garlic cloves, and a bunch of fresh, chopped cilantro. Consume with gusto! This treat is especially satisfying when coupled with freshly-baked cornbread, or better yet, slices of our own polenta.

"Our doctor . . . a good clove of garlic."
17th Century European

(And, obviously, a good bowl of chili!)

Garlic Lamb Chili

Serves 7–8
Ingredients:

1 1/2 lbs.	diced lamb shoulder
1 1/2 lbs.	diced pork shoulder
4 tbsp.	ground cumin
4 tbsp.	flour
to taste	salt and freshly ground black pepper
1/2 cup	vegetable oil
2 med.	chopped onions
2 tbsp.	fresh chopped garlic
2	chopped jalapeño peppers
1 cup	garlic cloves
2 cups	Pasilla Chili Paste (see below)
1 bunch	chopped cilantro
12 oz.	dark beer
1	28 oz. can chopped tomatoes

Preparation:

1. Place meat in bowl, toss in cumin, flour, salt, and pepper.
2. In a large, deep skillet or pot heat the oil and brown the meat.
3. Add the onion, chopped garlic, and jalapeño peppers. Sauté for 3 minutes.
4. Add all other ingredients and simmer for 1 1/2 hours, uncovered.
5. Skim fat from the top.
6. Serve with cornbread or Polenta (see recipe p. 55).

Pasilla Chili Paste
Ingredients:

10	Pasilla peppers
1/2 can	Chipotle chiles

Prepartion:

1. Place peppers in a saucepan and cover with water.
2. Bring to a boil and cook until soft.
3. Strain and save water.
4. Transfer to a bowl. Add Chipotle chiles. Puree with a hand blender.
5. Add saved water until desired consistency is reached.

Garlic Folklore

Garlic has been adored and abhored since ancient times . . .

And in Cuba, "thirteen cloves of garlic at the end of a cord, worn around the neck for thirteen days, was considered a safeguard against jaundice. But, on the thirteenth day, the wearer must go to the corner of two streets, take off his necklace and fling it behind him, and run home without seeing what became of it." (From "Plant Lore, Legends and Lyrics," by Folkard.)

Roman soldiers and Greek Olympic athletes believed garlic consumption would produce strength and courage.

Lots of cultures believed that when hung around the neck or placed above doorways in homes, garlic would ward off evil spirits, demons, misfortunes and VAMPIRES!

It also brought strength and stamina to the laborers who built the ancient Egyptian pyramids at Giza. Some notable Egyptians believed in its powers, too. King Tut was buried with it!

Chinese have used the herb for over 4,000 years. Earliest records show it was used as a food preservative.

Large supplies of garlic are purchased each year by the townspeople of Bologna, Italy, who regard it as a symbol of plenty and a charm against poverty during the year.

Original, ancient recipes have proven it—Mesopotamians used garlic in cooking!

Regarding it as "peasant food," historically English gentlemen never ate garlic.

Evil spirits were allegedly kept away from infants between birth and baptism if garlic was placed in the cradle during the Middle Ages.

Main Event
Garlic Steak Tartare

" The bullfighters of the Aymara Indian tribes of Bolivia carried garlic into the ring believing that the bull would not charge if he smelled it."

Well, wouldn't you? So much for the bull. Now, on to the beef . . .

ur Garlic Steak Tartare is the perfect cold-plate main course, or a perfect bite-size appetizer. Whenever and however you serve it, your guests will think you were locked in the kitchen for hours! We've prepared this dish with just the right amount of garlic and spices, resulting in this tangy, savory sensation, perfectly spreadable on toast points or crackers. And that's no bull!

Serves 4
Ingredients:

1/2 lb.	very lean beef (top round or filet)
1 tsp.	freshly chopped garlic
2 tbsp.	capers
1/4 cup	finely minced onion
1/4 cup	finely minced parsley
2 1/2 tsp.	Dijon mustard
2 tbsp.	olive oil
2 tsp.	Worcestershire sauce
1/4 tsp.	red pepper sauce
1	egg yolk
to taste	salt and freshly ground black pepper

Preparation:

1. Trim any fat from the meat. Chop in a food processor.
2. Place chopped meat in a bowl.
3. Add all other ingredients. Mix well.
4. Form into balls, garnish and serve with toast points.

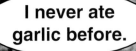

Is garlic good for the complexion?

I never ate garlic before.

Here is one of The Stinking Rose's customers!
Kristina Koprivawitch
before indulging in the herb.

Baccala Patate

*A*nother food celebrated by the Italian fishermen, or pescatori, was dried, salted codfish, or baccala. Detailing the pescatori's romantic yet rough life at sea, an article called "Italian Fisherman" appeared in the San Francisco Chronicle on July 20, 1885. Preparation for the fisherman's long sojourns at sea was called an "Italian labor of love." Ample quanties of bread, homemade red wine, and baccala sustained them during their days or even weeks at sea.

Why didn't they eat the fresh fish they caught? We'll never know. Maybe it's because baccala is even better!

Eating baccala, or a dish prepared with baccala, is also an Italian Christmas Eve tradition. But don't wait until then! You can try our dish at home, and your guests and family will certainly enjoy your own "labor of love."

Serves 5–6
Ingredients:

½ lb.	boneless, skinless salt cod
2 med.	boiling potatoes, peeled and cut up
⅜ cup	heavy cream
¼ cup	extra virgin olive oil
1 tsp.	freshly chopped garlic
to taste	salt and freshly ground black pepper
to taste	grated parmesan cheese

Preparation:

1. Soak the fish in fresh water for 1 day in the refrigerator. Change the water 3 times.
2. Place the cod in a saucepan. Cover with cold water and bring to a simmer. Remove from heat and let stand covered for 15 minutes.
3. Cook the potatoes in boiling water and drain.
4. Heat the cream and the olive oil.
5. In a food processor, add the cod and chopped garlic and pulse until combined.
6. Add the potatoes and continue to pulse until combined.
7. Add the cream and olive oil and pulse until combined.
8. Remove mixture and fill a gratin dish. Top with parmesan cheese and bake in a 450° oven until top is golden brown.
9. Serve with toasted, sliced baguette.

Polenta

hildhood memories of the Italian family are bound to include the sights and sounds of a large pot of polenta bubbling and popping on the stove under Mamma's careful supervision.

Today, many Americans enjoy variations of this traditional, comforting, staple food. Our version includes mozzarella cheese and a pinch of nutmeg to make it truly unique.

Serves 4–5
Ingredients:

1 qt.	water
1 cup	cornmeal
4 oz.	grated mozzarella cheese
1 tsp.	salt
1 pinch	nutmeg
1 tsp.	white pepper
1 tsp.	butter

Preparation:

1. In a 3-quart saucepan, bring the water to a boil.
2. Slowly stir in the cornmeal and lower heat to a simmer.
3. Continue to stir until cornmeal thickens and comes to a very smooth consistency, about 20 minutes.
4. Add cheese, salt, nutmeg, and white pepper.
5. Stir until cheese is combined.
6. Pour into a shallow cake pan and refrigerate.
7. When cool, cut into 1 x 4-inch pieces and fry in butter.

Garlic Crab Cakes

Here's another crabby creation that celebrates the culinary glory of San Francisco's king of crustaceans, the Dungeness Crab. You can, prepare our dish using other types of crab meat, but we're partial to the best! (We mean, the "local" kind . . .) Our crab meat is combined with fresh bell pepper, crisp red onion, savory spices and seasonings, and fried to a golden brown. Then it's crowned with a dollop of fresh Garlic Remoulade (see below) which you also create yourself. It's a dish certainly befitting royalty! And your own court, too, of family and friends.

Serves 3–4
Ingredients:

1 lb.	crab meat
1	red bell pepper, finely diced
1	green bell pepper, finely diced
1/2	red onion, finely chopped
3	eggs
1 tbsp.	freshly chopped garlic
1/2	jalapeño pepper, finely chopped
1/4 tsp.	red pepper sauce

2 tbsp.	mayonnaise
1/2 cup	fresh bread crumbs
1/2 cup	vegetable oil
1/2 cup	cornmeal

Preparation:
1. Combine all ingredients except oil and cornmeal.
2. Form mixture into 1/4 lb. patties.
3. Heat the oil in a large skillet.
4. Roll patties in the cornmeal and fry until golden brown on both sides.
5. Serve with Garlic Remoulade (see below).

Garlic Remoulade

And here it is, the key to the "crowning finish" for our Garlic Crab Cakes . . .(Of course, we think it's the *best* way to top off this particularly crabby treat.) And once you've prepared it yourself, we're sure you'll find many other occasions to "bestow royalty" upon even your most humblest of dishes!

Serves 4
Ingredients:

1 tsp.	Dijon mustard
1 cup	mayonnaise
1 tsp.	lemon juice
1/2	red onion, finely chopped
1 tsp.	finely chopped garlic
1/4 cup	finely chopped parsley
2	eggs, hard boiled and chopped

1 tbsp.	capers
to taste	salt, black pepper and cayenne pepper

Preparation:
1. In a bowl combine mustard, mayonnaise and lemon juice. Add remaining ingredients and season with salt, pepper, and cayenne.

It has been said that garlic keeps vampires away. Well, we can say unequivocally that . . .

Not one of our customers has ever been bitten.

Garlic Basil Custard

*H*ere are yet more additions that play wonderful supporting roles to some of our "Main Events," or perform well on their own. They are award-winners when helping you create a garlicky feast!

May I have the envelope (or, recipe) please . . .

Serves 6–7
Ingredients:

3 cups	milk
1/2 tsp.	freshly chopped garlic
6	eggs, whole
3	egg yolks
1/2 cup	freshly chopped basil
to taste	salt and pepper

Preparation:

1. Place milk and garlic in medium saucepan and bring to a boil.

2. Whip the eggs in a non-reactive bowl and while stirring, add scalded milk.

3. Process the basil and egg mixture in a food processor. Add salt and pepper to taste.

4. Strain through a fine mesh strainer and fill six 8 oz. ovenproof soufflé cups.

5. Place cups in a baking pan half-filled with hot water.

6. Bake at 325° for 1 hour or until a toothpick comes out clean when inserted into center of custard.

7. Let cool for 10 minutes. Run a paring knife around the edge of the custard, place a plate over the top of the cup, invert, and gently shake the custard onto the plate.

8. Serve with Marinara Sauce (see below).

Marinara Sauce

*I*t's another staple that no Italian kitchen ever goes without. Even though meat was always good and plentiful in the old country, Italians still craved and created a pasta sauce born of tomatoes and vegetables, simmered slowly to release the wonderful fragrance of tomatoes, herbs and spices throughout the house and, when including garlic, throughout the neighborhood as well. Our recipe, of course, includes garlic—enough to tantalize your nose as well as your taste buds *alla marinara!*

Makes 1 1/2 quarts
Ingredients:

1/2 cup	olive oil
4 med.	diced yellow onions
8 cloves	minced garlic
1 bunch	chopped fresh parsley
1 tsp.	crushed red chili pepper
2	28 oz. cans pear tomatoes in liquid
2	bay leaves
2 tsp.	anise seed

Preparation:

1. Heat the oil in a large pot. Sauté the onion.

2. Add garlic, parsley and red chili pepper. Sauté two minutes.

3. Add tomato, anise seed and bay leaves. Bring to a boil, then simmer for two hours.

VAMPIRE EXPOSED

LOVES TO EAT GARLIC

JANUARY 14 1964

THE GLOBAL INQUISITOR

LARGEST CIRCULATION OF ANY PAPER IN GILROY

AMAZING GARLIC DIET

LOVE TO BE THIN AND POPULAR (WE HAVEN'T WORKED OUT THE POPULAR YET). MORE ON PAGE 17

HEALTH CRISIS AWAITED HOSPITALS AND DOCTORS OFFICES INTERUPTED AS PEOPLE TURN TO GARLIC

SECRET GARLIC EATER TELLS ALL! TURN TO PAGE 25

THE SECRET TO MY SUCCESS

BY COUNTESS GARLICKA SEE PAGE 10

TRANSVALIA
R.I.P.

VAMPIRE COMES OUT OF CLOSET CASKET. WHEN I WAS YOUNG, ABOUT 700 YEARS AGO, I KNEW I WAS DIFFERENT SO I MOVED TO SAN FRANCISCO... CONTINUED PAGE 13

HUGE QUANTITIES OF GARLIC CONSUMED AT LOCAL RESTAURANT

TAKES OVER NEIGHBORHOOD

Little Extras

These two garlicky cocktail concoctions are popular libations among our patrons. Now you can "shake 'em up" at home!

Garlic Ramos Fizz
Serves 1
Ingredients:

3	sugar cubes
1/2 oz.	heavy cream
1/2 oz.	sweet & sour mix
1 oz.	orange juice
1 dash	garlic syrup
1 dash	soda water
1	egg
1 1/2 oz.	gin

Preparation:
1. Fill blender with ice.
2. Add all ingredients and blend.
3. Serve with orange slice.

Vampire Mary
Serves 1
Ingredients:

2 dashes	red pepper sauce
2 dashes	bitters
15 dashes	Worcestershire sauce
1/2 tsp.	prepared horseradish
1/4 tsp.	finely chopped garlic
15 dashes	salt
15 dashes	pepper
1/4	lime, juice squeezed
1/4	lemon, juice squeezed
1 1/2 oz.	vodka
6 oz.	tomato juice

Preparation:
1. Fill glass with ice.
2. Mix all ingredients and shake well.
3. Drink in the presence of a vampire.

Contrary to its name, our Vampire Mary will NOT attract vampires! (Attention all vampires: omit crushed garlic for your enjoyment.)

You may want to bypass the traditional glass of orange juice and opt instead for this "anytime" eye-opener!

Garlic Marinade

urn your meat and fish dishes into garlic masterpieces with this quick and easy marinade. Who knows—it may be the start of something big in your kitchen! "Let's see, what can I marinate next . . ." Watch out!

Serves 3
Ingredients:

³/₈ cup	freshly chopped garlic
1 finely	chopped yellow onion
2 tbsp.	chopped fresh thyme
4 tbsp.	chopped parsley
2 cups	Marinara Sauce (see recipe p. 59).

Preparation:
1. In a bowl combine all of the above and mix well.

Garlic Croutons

ou'll have to be careful with this recipe, too, because once you realize how simple it is to make these crunchy, munchy, seasoned tidbits at home, there will be no stopping you from sprinkling them *everywhere* to add garlicky, toasty taste to salads, vegetables, side dishes, soups . . . Oh noooo . .

Serves 7
Ingredients:

1	baguette
1 oz.	butter
¹/₈ cup	olive oil
1 tbsp.	chopped garlic
to taste	salt and pepper

Preparation:
1. Cut baguette into 1-inch cubes and place in a bowl.
2. Sauté together butter, olive oil, garlic, salt and pepper.
3. Pour over bread and toss well.
4. Place on cookie sheet and bake at 325° for 15–20 minutes or until light brown and crunchy.

"Since garlic hath powers to save from death/bear with it though it makes unsavory breath."

Salerno Regimen of Health (12th century)

Help! Bring the fresh parsley—quick!

hese next "little extras" are *Buon Apetito* from South of the Border! Mexican foods have become increasingly popular over recent years, and salsas come in as many variations as there are ways to enjoy them. We've taken one of the more popular versions of this chunky, fragrant sauce and made it The Stinking Rose® way—with lotsa fresh garlic! Your homemade version will be a popular and welcome addition to your next get-together, and your friends will appreciate the effort—which really isn't much at all!

Garlic Salsa with Fresh Tortilla Chips

Serves 5
Ingredients:

3	ripe tomatoes
1 med.	onion
1 tbsp.	freshly chopped garlic
1	fresh jalapeño pepper, seeded
1 bunch	cilantro
3	limes, juice squeezed
to taste	salt
1 tbsp.	olive oil
2 cups	vegetable oil
1 package	corn tortillas
to taste	garlic salt

Preparation:

1. Remove the stems of the tomatoes and finely chop.
2. Finely chop onion, garlic, and seeded jalapeño.
3. Chop cilantro and combine with above ingredients. Add lime juice and season with salt. Set aside.
4. Heat oil in a deep skillet (or pot) to 350°.
5. Cut tortillas into wedges and fry until crisp.
6. Drain chips well and sprinkle with garlic salt.
7. Serve chips with salsa.

Garlic Mayonnaise

*T*his sure isn't the kind of mayonnaise you'll find in a jar! Make it at home and make it fresh, and you'll notice the tasty, garlicky difference in salads or sandwiches. Be creative!

Serves 2–3
Ingredients:

6 cloves	peeled garlic
1	egg
1 tbsp.	light olive oil
to taste	salt and pepper

Preparation:

1. Chop garlic in food processor until very fine.
2. Add egg yolk and continue to process until smooth.
3. Add the olive oil slowly, a few drops at a time.
4. When all the olive oil is absorbed, season with salt and pepper.

Garlic Rose **Relish**

*T*he uses for this garnish are too numerous to mention! Always keep some on hand for your favorite garlic lover, and use your imagination to let our Garlic Rose Relish liven up your own creations.

Serves 6–7
Ingredients:

1 bunch	chopped parsley
¼ cup	chopped garlic
2 tbsp.	vinegar
1 tsp.	salt
olive oil to cover	

Preparation:

1. Mix parsley, garlic, vinegar and salt.
2. Add oil to cover ingredients. Stir.
3. Cover and store in refrigerator.

Garlic Potato Chips

y popular demand, and as luck would have it for all you fans of our restaurant, our Garlic Potato Chips are now on sale! Look for the bag that resembles our restaurant . If you don't get out much, have a friend pick up a fresh bag for you! Trust us: don't try to make them at home. Leave this one to us! Besides, the bag alone is a work of art!

Once you've tried this really nifty and delicious snack, and, if you really enjoy them, and we're quite certain you will, please tell your family, friends, people on the street, everyone! — that you've just eaten the most stinkingly good snack EVER!

The aromatic memories will linger long after the last crumb is consumed . . .

Garlic's "Medicinal" Folklore

• Garlic "kills worms in children, purges the head, helps lethargy, is a good preservative against and remedy for any plague, and takes away skin spots."
—Nicholas Culpeper

• Ancient cultures such as the Hebrews, Egyptians, Greeks, Romans and Asians used garlic as a medicinal remedy to treat and cure a wide variety of ailments.

• One of the earliest "healing" uses for garlic was as a treatment for heart ailments. It was found to be effective in slowing the process of heart disease by preventing and dissolving blood clots, and lowering blood pressure and cholesterol levels.

• The Berbers ground garlic and baked it in bread to be eaten for a cold. They also used the plant as an aid to conception. They added it to water as a disinfectant.

• Garlic was used as an antiseptic and an early antibiotic, whether applied directly to the wound, or consumed. It was used on the front lines of World War I by the British as an antiseptic dressing.

• The herb was believed to be an early antidote to poison and was used to treat bites and stings from animals and insects.

• It has been reported effective in killing various fungi and bacteria, and allegedly curbs the development of certain cancers and digestive ailments.

How about that!

Garlic Cough Syrup

ou won't find this prepa-
ration in any drugstore
even in our own "Little
aly" of North Beach) or dis-
ensed by any present day
harmacist, but, hey, we think
works pretty well! We'll
et that it can also keep away
contagious vampire or two!

*Our apothecary's shop is
ur garden full of pot herbs,
nd our doctor is a good
love of garlic."*

*— Poet unknown
A Deep Snow"
615*

Makes 1 ½ quarts
Ingredients:

1 lb.	sliced and peeled garlic cloves
3 tbsp.	braised fennel seeds
3 tbsp.	caraway seeds vinegar and sugar

Preparation:

1. Place garlic in a large pot with 1 quart of cold water.
2. Bring to a boil and cook until garlic is soft.
3. Add fennel and caraway seeds.
4. Cover and let stand for 12 hours.
5. Strain the liquid and add an equal amount of vinegar.
6. Bring to a boil and add enough sugar to make a syrup.
7. Take 2-3 tablespoons and call us in the morning!

The Big Finish
Garlic Ice Cream

*T*ime and time again, patrons of The Stinking Rose® look to this dessert selection on our menu and inquire, "Is there REALLY garlic in the ice cream?" You bet there is! It's just the right amount to make our Garlic Ice Cream the most stinkingly good (and likely the most unusual) dessert you've ever tasted! It's also a really cool (and creamy) way to top off a delightfully garlicky meal.

And now, our highly acclaimed and most famous sweet treat, Garlic Ice Cream.

Serves 4–5
Ingredients:
3 cups	whole milk
¼ tsp.	freshly chopped garlic
1	vanilla bean, split in half
1 cup	heavy cream
1½ cups	granulated sugar
9	egg yolks

Preparation:
1. Put milk, garlic and vanilla in a saucepan. Bring to a boil and remove from heat.
2. In a mixing bowl blend cream, sugar and egg yolks.
3. Strain the scalded milk mixture into the egg and sugar mixture, stirring constantly.
4. Return the combined mixture to the pan and stir continuously over moderate heat until it coats the back of a spoon, about 10–15 minutes.
5. Cool in an ice bath.
6. Freeze until firm.

Credits & Acknowledgments

Now that we've tantalized your taste buds, educated you about our favorite "herb," made you chuckle and smile, what more do you want? Another Stinking Cookbook? Well, hold on — it's been fun, but not that much fun! (I'm kidding, of course!) Let's digest this one for a while, but for the future, who knows. In the meantime, you can enjoy all these fabulous recipes, our take-home products and snacks, and, of course, The Stinking Rose®, our unique garlic restaurant.

I'd like to thank the many folks who helped put this stinking idea on paper, and who helped bring our dishes to life on these pages. Without their help (and with their help, I guess) this book TRULY STINKS!

Jerry Dal Bozzo

Special thanks to our:

Writer
Karen Wegrzyn

Designer/Illustrator
Marlene Bauer-Holder

Book Producer
Dean Dal Bozzo

Photographer
Derrick Dobbs

Recipe Developer
Rob Larman

Recipe Tester
Linda Butler

Food Stylist
Kelvin Ott

Photo Models
Kristina Kopriva
pp. 51, 58, 60
Ralph Giovanniello
p. 50
Dean Dal Bozzo
p. 58, 60
Pam Dal Bozzo
p. 60
Angelo Ferrari
p. 40

Contributors
Chuck Kennedy
Miranda Gonsalves
Marsha Garland
Bill Strange
Gilroy Garlic Festival
Melvin Belli
Senator Quentin Kopp
The Smothers Brothers
Lyle Tuttle Photo is by
Jock McDonald

According to the Stinking Rose™:
Use garlic all the time!

76

Stinking Notes

Stinking Notes

Stinking Notes

Stinking Notes